C000082637

4:04_AM_ Thoughts

POETRY BY

BARBARA GIANQUITTO

4:04AM Thoughts

All rights reserved, including the right to reproduce this book, or portions thereof in any form. No part of this text may be reproduced, transmitted, downloaded, decompiled, reverse engineered, or stored, in any form or introduced into any information storage and retrieval system, in any form or by any means, whether electronic or mechanical without the express written permission of the author.

© 2021 **Barbara Gianquitto**

Illustrations and cover by: Elizabeth Spary

Editor: Stefanie Briar

Photography: Federica Barbiero

To my late mother Silvana,
you gave me my words.

These are all for you

Contents

Introduction

I believe in the power of serendipity, and that this book
is in your hands now for a reason.
I see poems as messages in a bottle, picked up almost by
accident to discover something you needed just at that
time. Something powerful and thought provoking.

Becoming an author has been my dream for many years,
and I have expressed myself through writing since I was
thirteen. I use my pen as a medicine at times, as I find
writing somewhat cathartic.

The title *4:04AM Thoughts* comes from the time of the
night I often wake up, as if by someone else, with a mes-
sage I had to pay close attention to.

I later discovered that 404 represents an angel number as
a way for the universe to convey a message of persever-
ance, and an urge to never give up, as you truly can achieve
anything you wish.

As soon as I had decided to put my poems into a book, I stopped waking up at 4:04am, and so I took that as a sign that I was on the right path!

4:04AM Thoughts is a collection of poems, about heartbreak, love, death, joy, and motherhood; about a world that needs more kindness and a woman that never gave up.

My message is one of hope and resilience, and journey into finding myself and all the different versions of me; to love them whole for what they were, what they are now and what they will become.

Between life and death
there is always a debt.
Light will shine on you,
but through all the pain
you must go through,
don't despair (as things will repair).
This journey, I agree,
is not always fair.
But with courage at hand,
the road will reveal
the beauty of lessons
in every ordeal.

A lucid dream

Poetry

The way you look at me.
The way you make me feel whole.
The way you make me feel safe.
This, to me, is poetry.

Love

A soul is a time traveller.
There are no limits,
and no schemes
or infrastructures.
Souls are not bound
to hard logic or rules.
A soul always knows
just where it belongs;
and a soul will not stop its journey
until they are finally home.
It might take them one year,
or one thousand, or one million.
Or it might just be the amount of time
it takes us to take just one
deep and loving sigh.

Silence and wildflowers

I crave touch and smiles,
and to wake up to
warm hugs and soft kisses.
I long for sharp clarity of mind
and gentle reassurances.
I yearn for soothing silence,
and head strokes,
and rainbows, and wildflowers.
I am forever wishing for
a simpler time.

Untwine me

Untwine me.
Unravel me.
Untangle me.
Break these chains
my heart is trapped inside.
Whisper some words I can believe,
and quiet this raging storm inside me.
Love my broken pieces.
Breathe away the pain.
Free my soul.

Look at me

Look at me in a way that
you really see me.
In a way you reach my soul.
Like you know how to.
Look at me.
Don't hold back.
Say what you feel.
Say it more.
Say it too much.
Don't half live.
Don't half feel.
Don't half say.
In the end this is what counts.
We won't remember why we cried or laughed.
We will remember the way we held each other
during difficult times.
Look at me.
Don't close your eyes.
Don't let the unspoken words be louder.
Live your feelings.
Give them life.
Give them words.
Give them oxygen.
We are here today.

And we may not be
tomorrow.
Everything else is just a convention.
Just metal barriers all around.
But we are above that.
Look at me.
See where we are.
So far away.
Who says we have to live like everybody else?
Who says that is the right way?

Look at me.
Does it feel right?
Can you feel my heart beating
beside yours?

Rest your head on my chest.
I'm holding you.
Breathe.
Breathe again.
We are not as in control
as we might think.
But who really cares?
Look at me.
Does it feel right?

Just us

Sit with me;
just us.
Let's talk
until the world
doesn't feel scary anymore.

The circle of life

People will come and go from our lives.
This is inevitable, and almost never about
something we have done.
People outgrow people and values change;
so do perspectives and interests.
Illnesses take centre stage
and sweep our loved ones away.
Life happens, and stops, and changes.
It always changes.
As life evolves, so do we.
So be gentle with yourself.
If you do nothing else at all today,
please do that.

Tangling lights

I can't see the beginning of us,
nor the end...
much like a ball of intertwined lights,
always shining and tangled,
and somehow
always together.

The magic wand

If I could wave the magic wand,
I would be with you.
I would wake with you each day.
I would never stop smiling.
I would be grateful to have found you.
And I would be even more grateful
to have you as my own.

If I could wave the magic wand,
there would be no hurt.
There would be no more tears.
There would be no resentment.
There wouldn't be anyone crying for us.
I would have found a way
for all of us to be happy.
To be content.

If I could wave the magic wand,
I wouldn't want anything more or anyone else.
I would love you, as I never thought possible.
I would cry tears of happiness, and only happiness.
I would even forget what the word "sadness" even means.

If I could wave the magic wand,

I would ask for your happiness.
I would ask that all your dreams come true.
I would ask for your path to be lit
so you may walk without stumbling.
I would ask that when you close your eyes at night,
you do so with a smile on your lips,
so you can say with truth
"I have everything my heart desires."

Surrender

What is love
if not the surrender
of all expectations?
What is love
if not the belief
that for every winter that ends,
a new spring is ripening
around the corner?
What is love
if not the hope that,
this time,
spring will last
just a little longer?

No more music

You shut me off like a song
you no longer want to hear.
I felt like a wounded animal,
howling and crawling
against the bare floor.
I felt my skin burning,
and my very bones shattering
one by one.
I could almost see the scene from afar,
as though I was no longer
in my own body.
And all that was left,
were the scattered pieces
of who I once was.

Love and coffee

It was something resembling love;
that kiss on the forehead,
those hugs in the kitchen,
that coffee in the bed in the morning,
and that sense of being whole.
When we were the only two people
in the entire universe itself,
it was something *resembling* love.

Moonlight

Wherever you are now
my love,
know that we can still see
the very same moon
whilst counting
the same wild stars.

If I could

If I could only have one last word,
I would want to hear yours.
If I could only have one more kiss,
I would want only yours.
If I could only have one last hug,
I would ask for your embrace.
If I could only see one last smile,
it would, of course, be yours.
If I could only hear one bout of laughter,
it would naturally be yours.
If I could only choose one final trip,
I'd want to come to you.
Up in the clouds where I imagine you
happy and smiling.
I hope my words will reach you there;
carried by gentle feathers,
whispering nothing less
than eternal love.

A beautiful disaster

We made such a mess of this love,
you and I...
forever
the most
beautiful disaster.

Running

Running toward the shining light,
feeling restless;
gasping for air.
Running, running to be sure
that the light won't fade.
Running to grab and hold it,
to be fully certain
it will not and cannot ever go away.
Hungrily consuming each other's minds,
each other's bodies,
and each other's hearts,
in the attempt to feel that void
that grows by the day.
The more we are together,
the more we want to be together.
More, more, more.
Never enough.
A new beginning on the horizon,
It seems so far and yet so near.
Running towards our feelings
like reckless children,
we carry patience we do not have.
We hold passion that consumes us.

Each discovery brings a new way
to rethink the past.
Take my hand.
Breathe with me.
Breathe some more.
We are here.
Close your eyes
and feel my heart beating.

Nothing else matters.

What love is after all?

You translate my silences,
understanding what I need,
before I even say a thing.
You anticipate my smiles,
and accept my world
by becoming part of it.
You erase time and space.
And maybe, just maybe,
that is exactly what
love is after all...

You

You'll either be my new beginning,
or the absolute
end of me.

The wreckage

Through the ashes,
I found myself
in the dirt buried there;
deep in the mud,
and in the burnt flesh
that the wreckage of
your love has left.
I have found myself again,
holding the courage
I had lost,
and love for myself
I didn't know
that I deserved.
And I never want to
 lose me again...

not for love,
not for validation,
and not for
anything or anyone else
ever again.

Fear and faith

For every *what if*
fear screamed inside her head,
faith kept whispering
into her soul:
"So what?"

The day I said goodbye

Darkness is swallowing me whole,
as life slowly leaves your aching body,
and I wonder if your soul
has already left?
Can you hear me?
Can you feel me at all?
The day I held your hand for the last time,
as your eyes closed forever,
my heart broke beyond repair.
Could you hear the sound it made
as it cracked open?
I will find you again, in the next life.
This I promise.
Soulmates are not just lovers.
They are also those souls
that meet us again and again
in every lifetime,
re-joining and remembering.
You were mine, mum.
Fly free.
I will see you again.

Needy

They told her
she was needy,
and they told her
she was too much.
They told her
she was a handful,
and worst of all,
she ended up believing them.

Melting ice

I feel the ice
around my heart melting
from your words.
The unspoken ones.
The ones you speak with your eyes,
and ones your embrace
whispers to my heart.
They speak of eternal love,
and of *holiness*
and *sacred space*.

Breathe

Every smile that we manage
is a blessing,
and every tear is necessary
for our growth.
The right decision is the one
that comes without drama
and only a sense of peace.
It might be that it's not happening soon though...
and this only means that we are not yet ready
or that the timing is not on our side.
All we need to do is breathe
through this bad day,
and give our brains a break.
There is always tomorrow.
There is always tomorrow.

A smile

It was a smile.
His eyes smiled at me
even before his mouth did.
It was a moment;
the moment when
I recognised a soul.
Familiar, comfortable,
a feeling of needing to catch up
and tell each other everything
that had happened in all that time
we'd been apart.
A soothing voice reverberates
from my ears
and down into my heart,
speaking so softly.
I want to feel closer now,
but he is just a stranger.
My words flow almost uncontrolled,
sharing life stories, drinking coffee
and secretly wishing we could stop time.
I want to listen; listen to everything he's saying.
I can't miss any words.
I don't know how it happened,
but I wanted to be in his arms.

His eyes looking at me,
looking through me,
deep inside.
But he is a stranger.
And yet, through his words
a familiar sense of belonging
fiercely emerges,
telling me I've known him before,
telling me this is the moment
I have been waiting for.
I want to tell him I missed him,
but how can I do this
if I do not know him?
The strangest of feelings,
overwhelming desire of being held,
tight so tight I can't breathe.
It was a smile, that's how it started.
The sweetest and loving smile I've ever seen.
And he was smiling for me,
and suddenly he wasn't a stranger anymore.

Memories

Memories of you swirl in my mind
like white feathers
floating upon the air.
I try to catch them,
but the more I try,
the more they move away,
the way you did.

The blue shirt

I loved that colour of your shirt;
blue like your eyes.
As deep as the sea.
Looking down into me.
Oh, I want to be in your arms.
I have been waiting for you.
I'm being pulled like a magnet.
Keep looking at me.
Don't ever take it away.

The poisoned cup

I drank from the poisoned cup,
and the sweet venom
quenched my thirst,
my insides burning with every sip,
only to leave me wanting
more and more.
Only to leave me stripped down
and naked of my own self-worth.

Do not give up

It's okay to feel scared.
It's okay to feel lost.
it's okay to struggle.
it is simply okay.
You are okay.
This I promise.
Do not give up.
Trust that your heart will heal,
while choosing possibility
over infeasibility.
Ditch logic and odds
and hold on to
hope.

Thoughts

Only in the confusion did I find clarity.
Only in the mist did I find focus.
Only in the mud did I find myself.

Toward the water

She walked toward the water,
her feet sulking in the sand.
She was utterly stuck,
unable to step forward.
She couldn't reach the water,
yet so desperately wanted to.
The smell of that salty sea,
and tears streaming down her face.
The water was so calm,
so why didn't she feel the same?
Throat closing and hands tingling,
the cool wind against her face.
She closed her eyes and allowed the sun
to dry the tears.
She walked towards the water
so maybe one day
she will finally reach it.

The flower

This time of year, spring is showing all its true colours.
Flowers are blossoming with petals
that are bigger and brighter.
Only a few months ago they were so small.
Almost invisible.

This got me thinking, what happens if we want a flower
to blossom quicker?
Could we give it more water?
Should we expose it to more sun?
Then what would happen?
A flower exposed to too much water would die.
A flower exposed to too much light would blossom quickly
– like it happens sometimes during summertime – but
then it would burn just as fast and its petals would shatter
to wilted pieces.

A flower needs its time
to be what it is supposed to be.
It needs the natural elements.
It needs the right balance of sunlight and shade.
It needs the right balance of water and dryness.
It needs nurturing and patience
to truly blossom into its magnificence:

For it to survive.
For it to be truly appreciated.
I see the flower as love.

We cannot quicken the process.
We need to embrace those periods of shades
so that we can appreciate the light.
We need to nurture it
and wait till nature rides its course.
We cannot risk to burn it.
We cannot risk to drown it.
We want it to blossom.
We want to see the true work of the universe
all in one flower.

For this is the most beautiful flower,
and it is so precious.

I cannot wait until all the petals are out

reaching and blooming.

And I cannot wait
to smell the unique scent
and lose myself in such beauty
and remind myself that
we did allow the right balance
and we were so patient.

We were anticipating the sweet scent
and we nurtured it
and protected it
even when the petals were so small.
For we knew the potential
and we were not wrong.

We were not wrong.

Shortfalls

You only accept the love
you think you deserve.
Do not ever lower your value
to match someone else's shortfalls.
So aim for the stars,
beautiful soul.
What you want
awaits you.

Riding the waves

Riding the waves –
I hold onto the ocean of emotions
that are now submerging me.
Can you control the wild seas?
Can you still the storm that rocks this boat?
All we can do is to hold on,
and keep breathing,
riding the waves back
toward the calm.
You can easily fall.
You can easily drown.
Oh, but if you don't?
What if the storm was only needed
to show us the deep beauty of clear waters?
The silence,
the serenity,
the sun finally shining
against our closed eyes...
Peace.
At last.

The virginity of my soul

I want you to sit with me;
I want you to talk to me
until I am no longer frightened.
I want you to love my broken pieces.
I want you to love me
at my worst.
I want you to hold me gently
like I am going to break.
I want you to restore
the virginity of my soul.

Let's go for a walk

Take my hand,
and let's go for a walk.
Step out of the castle
and enclosed prison.
Just for a short while,
let's walk the unknown path.
You know the one;
we don't know where it leads,
yet we will turn towards
a beautiful flower,
and examine the colour,
the scent,
and the shape.

The grass stretches all around us.

Let's stop by a lake
and talk of the water's stillness.
Let's speak for hours
about the soft shapes of clouds...
laughing at ridiculous things,
breathing in all the sweet things.
Let's live in a made-up world,
a world we'd love to exist in.

Let us be pure energy.
Let us be fresh air.
Let it be us.
Let our hearts beat as fast as they desire.
Let's not ask anything.
Let's not plan anything.
Let it be only us,
in a world nobody knows about,
in a parallel universe
where nothing else matters
before we step in the material reality
where you and I live at the opposite sides of life.
Let us wait
'til we can see the flowers again.
Let it be us.

Never broken

Here I am, thinking of you again.
My mind wonders,
my soul reaches for you,
and my heart aches.

A connection that's never broken,
not even by the *silence*.

In every moonlight

I have searched for you in dreams,
and kept looking for you
in every moonlight,
following all the signs.
And I will continue to do so
until you are finally
here in my arms.

Blossoming

I move toward you like a sunflower
moves toward the sun.
You are my light.
You are my oxygen.
I blossom
and blossom,
basking in the warmth
of your love.

A new storm is coming.
I feel it in my bones,
and I am unprepared.
I don't have shelter,
and I am fighting
this battle I will lose
all alone.
All I can do is create memories
with this little time we have left.
Hold me now,
as I am breaking
like glass
while you see me
as a solid rock
in stormy seas.
I am not the rock.
I am the storm.

Breaking like glass

Mum

The seed you planted in me,
filled with wisdom,
resounds from my ears to my heart
constantly, every day.
I feel you are close to me;
your space in my heart
has never been replaced.
You taught me the importance of kindness,
how the light always filters
through even long shadows,
and that only in the broken pieces
I can finally be whole again.
You taught me that endings are just new beginnings
in the shape of pain and despair.
You taught me that flowers blossom in muck,
 gifting me the strength to carry on.
I didn't know I had to let it last a lifetime
when you left this world, Mum.
You gave me my words,
and so, *these are all for you.*

In solitude

And maybe, just maybe
it is not about waiting
for someone to save us.
It is about the ability
to truly believe that
we can do so ourselves.

It has always been you

Impossible to go back,
and unable to move forward,
in a place somewhere between,
sits our world;
where it is neither night nor day,
where nothing makes sense,
and yet, everything does.
We are stuck between now and forever.
It has always been you.
It has always been you.

Closing love

I wanted you to love me.
Simply me:
My flaws, my insecurities,
and my deepest scars.
I wanted you to see me,
and cherish me,
and all throughout, I didn't realise
I was looking for love;
the love I was
denying myself.

Where have I been?

I was forged into the woman I am now.

I was shown what I would
eventually not accept any longer.
I was going through the pain of giving without receiving to
then be capable of appreciating selfless acts when they'd
eventually arrive.

I was being taught that kindness is the most powerful
weapon you will ever have in life, by seeing and living
the opposite.

I was being challenged and made to believe I was not good
enough, so that I could really appreciate what it would
mean to be loved for exactly who I am.

I was cherishing and learning the wonders of motherhood.
I was learning to say goodbye- the one that rips your heart
straight out.
I was learning what a true loss is so that I could give per-
spective to closing a relationship without the heartache
of death.

I was learning that in life you either grow together or you
grow apart;
that nothing survives without truly understanding what
the other person needs above everything else.

Had I not gone through what I have, I wouldn't be who
I am today:
I wouldn't have my daughters.
I wouldn't care so much for somebody hurting.
I wouldn't be able to appreciate the value of somebody
asking how I am, and genuinely waiting for my answer.
I wouldn't know what not to accept as I wouldn't really
know what to look for.

So I am grateful for what I have gone through and will not
regret it, for as much as it has hurt me, it has made me a
better person.

Simple things

All I ever wanted was to be seen and heard
and for you to show up.
Tell me -
what was so difficult about that?

Missing the world

I miss the simple things:

A coffee shop chat with a stranger,
and driving in the sunshine.
The freedom to go where I want,
the children's laughter in a play centre,
and seeing your smile without a mask.

I miss the touch.
I miss the hugs.
I miss a simpler world.

Growth

I see her:
That version of myself.

I see her fears and her strengths.
I see what she believed in
and what she longed to be.
The reflection in the mirror now
gives me a distorted image,
but I will honour myself,
and what I *believe in now*.

28 - 3 - 2014

I remember that day:
I knew it was going to be the last time
I ever saw you.
My heart was heavy,
just as it is today.
I remember that day
like a movie in slow motion.
The sun was shining.
Oh, the sweet irony.
I remember saying 'it is such a beautiful day to die'.
I thought it would rain...
but the day I said goodbye to you,
It was the most beautiful day.

I guess the sky was ready
to welcome you home, my love.

Let your soul remember

And just when you feel you have nothing left to give,
and are abandoning ship,
life throws you a lifeboat
and surrounds you in the most beautiful of rainbows.
The rain is now drying,
and the light is finally shining from within.
Grab on to that;
carry it, hold it so close.
Take the lifeboat.
Soon you'll be swimming faster now,
riding the waves in full control
while enjoying the wind, soft against your face.
The pain disappears, and all you have left
is the wisdom that had left you.
The more painful the experience
the more powerful the lesson.
In your darkest moments, do remember this:
that it is only phase, and will not last forever.
You can do this, you already have in all your lifetimes, let
your soul remember and guide you.

Lost in you

I'm looking at you.

I see you.
I see through you.
I feel your heart beating.
I feel the warmth
of your skin against mine.
I keep gazing at you beside me
as you return the gaze so deeply.
I feel you are reaching me
like nothing I've known.
And we are not speaking,
as the silence is worth more
than skies of tumbling words
as love doesn't have to be explained,
only felt.

So feel my heart.
Feel my embrace.
Relax into me.
Abandon yourself
into me.
I will not let you fall.
I will not let you fall.

As I kiss you softly
and we entwine once more to be one again,
I'm completely lost in you.
I've now found myself in you.

So feel my heart.
Feel my embrace.
Relax into me.
Abandon yourself
into me.
I will not let you fall.
I will not let you fall.

Freezing time

I want to stay in bed a little longer this morning.
I want to smell that familiar coffee,
and snuggle in your arms.
This is the world where everything makes sense.
The world where all my journeys end.

I want time to freeze always,
right there.

Hope

And one day we will finally make sense of it all.
A greater understanding.
A full view.
Until then, all we can do is to hold on
to *hope*.

You miss from me

I miss you in ways I didn't think
it could be humanly possible
to miss someone.
My heart aches,
and my bones are longing.

You are *missing from me*.
A piece has been ripped out.

They say time heals all wounds,
but I am not sure of that.
I am just waiting until the time
I can get used to the space you left,
and for the scar to form
to protect a wound
that will never heal...

More

I want more time,
so I can get a little bit more of you.
More of this love.
More of our slow dances together in the kitchen.
More of our silly laughter and jokes
that nobody else quite gets.
More of our endless conversations,
about everything and nothing.
I want more time,
before all that is left are memories.
Now that my heart is still whole,
I want more time.

Magic

Lavender and pinecones,
soaking in the warmth of your smile,
and drinking peppermint tea
surrounded by stardust
feels like magic.

Under water

My head is underwater,
and my body aches
as though a piece has been
forcefully removed
with no anaesthesia;
Brutally and intentionally.

You left me on my knees gasping for air,
without a small or single word.
You took this piece of my heart
along with you
and it wasn't yours to rip out
or run with.

All of me wasn't enough for you.
It never was.

Behind the clouds

When the sky is dark
and the clouds are angry,
crying the heaviest tears,
know that the sun is still shining,
somewhere just beyond the clouds.
Its rays are warming the droplets of rain
so they can evaporate,
and let the clouds dissipate
 to reveal the beautiful blue skies...
the exact same sky
where the clouds sit now.
It won't take long.
It is true after all that without rain,
there wouldn't be rainbows.

Peace

Peace at last:
Light at the end of the tunnel.
Out of the darkness and breathing.
For a small word, "peace" means the world;
A world yet to be unfolded,
a door yet to be opened, but you know that it is now
not as far away from you as it was before.
You're breathing even deeper
hoping that the other shoe won't drop.
Can we truly be happy, bright, and shiny?
Or do we constantly look for problems
so that once they've resolved,
we can have a sense of accomplishment?
Why can't we just be happy with what we have here?
What we have now?
The light is now filtering through on the grass,
and the rain is only enhancing the colours.
Yes, I can see colours now.
Yet, long will it last?

The last Christmas

This love trapped inside me
doesn't find release
in bells ringing for Christmas.
If I knew it was going to be the last one,
I would have kissed you more often,
and hugged you even tighter.
I would have said I love you
'till you asked me to stop.
We thought we could fight this illness
we thought we were invincible...
And so I close my eyes
and let out a silent whisper
hoping it will reach you
wherever you are..

I wasn't looking for you

This is new.
This is unexpected.
I wasn't looking for you.
I wasn't looking for anything.
Then you gazed at me.
Seeing deep down inside.
Reaching places no one else had.
Lifting a veil to show me something.
Something I hadn't known existed.
Something I couldn't quite define.
Something I still cannot comprehend.
I should be scared really.
For I have been hurt so much before.
But this is somehow not scary.
This doesn't sting.
This is healing.
This is comforting.
This is exciting.
This is gently bringing me back to life.
I always thought,
"When it's real you'll know;
as you will not be confused."
And I feel strangely confident, and bizarrely comfortable.

A weird sense of having found something lost
long ago.
Logic dictates that I shouldn't feel this way.
But, maybe, this is not about logic.
Maybe this is something else.
Something else altogether.

No more

I offer no explanations on how
I choose to repair what you broke.
I make no apology for wanting human contact that has
been denied for far too long.
For allowing myself to open up again.

I forbid you and anyone else
to clip my wings ever again.
I know my worth now.
I know who I am now.
So, you may hit me again with your words,
but I choose to not give them importance.
You are powerless.
You have no control over me anymore.
I can finally *breathe* again.

Fly free

The very essence
of what I thought broke me
made me grow.
All those dark nights,
spent in despair
gave me new light to follow
and jumping into the unknown.
I thought I'd hit against
the sharpest of rocks and bleed,
not realizing at the time
that was actually growing wings
to finally fly free.

Surviving

How am I, you ask?
I am surviving.
I am focusing on my next breath,
the next minute, the next hour
and then the next day.
I scrape for droplets of energy
and write my intentions
to the next full moon.
My intention is to carry on
and dance in the flames,
to somehow come out stronger.
But to do that, I need to first be able
to see how many pieces there are
to place *back together*.

Power

I am power in a vulnerable body.
I am the raging fire draped in sweetness.
I am a slow dance in a chaotic world.
I am the breeze of spring you long for.
I am the mother of everything
that is both good and pure.
I fight like a girl.
I always have,
and *always will*.

The last conversation

I don't need that last conversation.
I don't need to understand exactly what went wrong.
Your silence explained enough.

Barbara

I am a myriad of contradictions,
feeling too much and saying too little.
Loving me is easy
and also complicated.
I forgive but never forget.
Yet, I will show you the universe
and count the stars with you.

Backpack

She took all the courage she had left,
filled an imaginary backpack with
all her hopes and dreams,
and went on to *change a few things*.

Nothing breaks like the heart

But what about broken promises,
broken expectations,
broken hopes and
broken dreams?
What about the broken image
of the life we could have had?
The life we could have felt?
The life we could have seen?

Earth energy

Today I will be gentle with myself,
and speak with kindness.
I will soak in the soft energy of the earth,
and let her once again remind me
that resting is necessary
to replenish my soul.

I was always yours

I was always yours
through all the pain and tears.
I was always yours
through the silence,
and distance.
I was always yours,
but you were never mine.

The sacred garden

I am going to my happy place to rest. There is a stairwell there; a wooden one from a very dark place which I never understood. What is it? And where does it come from?

The stairs end in a beautiful garden as I step in.

I immediately look up at the sky. It is warm and there's a calming light made of purplish pink. It is soft yet bright enough. It's neither day or night but the space in between.

There are many stars and two moons, and I stop for a second to try and understand, soon realizing that this is not the time to apply any kind of rationale.

The smell is of fresh flowers and pinecones, and there is only one big tree on the right of the garden, and a little pond with a little bridge on top.

I breathe in the silence and the peace with only the tranquil sound of water trickling into the pond. I take deep comfort in knowing that I am here once again in a place where I cannot be hurt.

I walk to my favourite spot on the wooden bench, just near the little pond. I have rested on that bench countless times.

I sit with bare feet, sulking into the fresh grass while absorbing the energy that rises from the ground.

It is there where I replenish my energy, get lost in that beautiful purple sky, and – for just a little while – forget all about the world.

Soulmates

Let me tell you a story,
of when my eyes first met yours
and I saw a galaxy
of a million possibilities.
Let me tell you that story
of when I felt I recognised you
from another life.

Sit with me,
let me tell you that story.

The past

The past is ringing its bell,
luring me into the abyss of memories,
and forcing them to resurface.
The past is ringing its bell
and making such loud noise,
disturbing the sweet tranquillity
of my newfound soul at peace.
The past which was once my present,
is a reality made of heartbreak and lies
that I am not answering now.
Not this time.
I am leaving it just
where it belongs,
For it has *nothing* new to say.

I feel you

I feel your silence.
I feel your distance.
I feel your worry.
I feel how torn you are.
I feel how you cannot breathe.
I feel your need for relief.
If I could, I'd give your soul shelter.
If I could, I'd erase your worries.
If I could, I'd lie with you on the grass so we can feel the
earth together.
I'd stay with you until you become clear again.
I'd hold you until your tears are emptied and dry.
I'd kiss you softly, whispering that all will
eventually be okay.
If I could, I'd talk to you until the world
no longer feels frightening.
If I could, I'd light your path and smile
whilst seeing you walking it with confidence.
There are no easy answers,
only the complexity of life.
Every smile in one world is a tear in the other.
Balancing is almost impossible, I know.
But we'll keep holding hands
whilst we navigate the storm.

You beat inside me now.

You are part of me.

Your hurt is mine.

Your happiness is mine.

There is no middle ground, only the pure and unselfish
desire for the other person to be well.

And if you drift off away from me,

as life turns its tables,

please remember to try and hear my voice

through any tears and anger,

echoing the sweet words of eternal love.

Lullabies

She is a lullaby in a night storm.
She is the star that lights your path.
She is the moon that holds your secrets.
She is the gentle river
you sit beside
whenever you are sad.
And she is the campfire that warms you
through the coldest nights.

March winds

The March winds are sweeping me away,
and the winter in my heart is not disappearing.
How can I say goodbye to everything
that is so pure and beautiful?
I could ask 'why'? a million times,
and the only answer I will ever hear
is the sound of the hounding wind
and the crashing waves
of an ocean of emotions
that are now drowning me.

I can't breathe here under water.

The answer

The answer is always somewhere
never too far;
in the smiles of strangers,
the quotes you find by chance,
in the unexpected compassion
of someone you've never known,
and in the poignant questions from children.

The universe always works its magic.
We just have to be ready to listen.

Please breathe and listen.

The moon and the cloud

There is a sweet and melancholic light
covering the moon tonight.
She is feeling so lonely,
that loses herself in that
distant embrace with the sun,
feeling his warmth without touching him,
and knowing his energy without seeing him.
Oh, how she would love to feel that eclipse once again,
when she was perfectly aligned with the sun
locked in a flawless embrace,
in complete harmony.
She knows it will be a long time
'till she can feel this again.
And somehow this is enough;
enough for her to continue to shine
in the dark night.

Flames

You made love to my mind and soul,
igniting the red flames
only to let the fire burn as you walked away,
as though you never existed.
You watched those flames turn into ashes
returning to their nothingness.

What was that for?

Lies

They were lies,
lies that felt like warm honey
dripping on strawberries.
Like water after chocolate,
and a shower of rainbows,
and sweetest lullabies.
The ones you can't resist falling asleep
with a smile on your face to.
Yes, they were lies, but oh...
How sweet they did sound...

This is me

Don't ask me to pace myself,
for I cannot do it.
Don't ask me to take things slowly,
for I don't know what it means.

I wear my heart on my sleeve and I give it all I have.
It doesn't matter if I get hurt.
Life is too short – way too short.
It doesn't matter if my heart falls in the wrong hands,
for it is so easy to grab.
I prefer to say what I think,
and share what I feel exactly when I feel it.

Live every moment to the fullest.

Don't ask me to distance myself.
Don't ask me to be afraid of what I feel.
Don't let the words die in my mouth.
I may not be here tomorrow, and my words will live on.
You either get all of me or none.

This is me.
Would you ask a hurricane to spare this house
or that car or those trees?

Some hurricanes come to clear the path.
So enjoy what you get,
and lose yourself in the madness.
but don't ask me to slow down.

This is me, and I'm worth it.

Stars

Find me where the stars fall
and catch me
every time.

Everywhere

I have walked everywhere.
I have walked for what feels like one thousand miles.
I have walked on the crossroads
and pathways of my mind.
I have seen some dark paths,
I have seen many thorns,
and I have seen gates closed
as I've walked on muddy roads.
I have seen footprints next to mine,
and I have seen many disappear along the journey.
I have seen some steady just ahead.
I wonder if they led my journey for a little while.
I wonder if I followed the correct ones.
I have seen flowers battered,
and petals scattered around.
I have walked in the rain
watching my steps...
I have not looked up to the sky
for the longest time,
as the rain has been too heavy.
I have stopped and looked at a crossroad,
and have chosen a different path;
one where I caught myself in thorns
that made me bleed.

This is the only one where I can see
a glimpse of sunshine at the end.
I am walking alone, but I am no longer scared.
There will be new footprints next to me,
and I will be looking toward the sky again.
The clouds will move.
The rain will stop.
I can see at the end of the path a beautiful flower,
just waiting for the sun to dry the drops of rain
from its soft petals.
I just have to keep walking.

Spring

I am ready for the winter in my heart
to make space for spring.
I long for the day I can *blossom* again.

Missing me?

I am not that person anymore.
The one who would stroke your ego.
The one who would put you on a pedestal.
The one who would put your needs first.
You had an ocean in me
and you turned your back to it.
You say you miss me now,
yet when you had me,
I wasn't enough for you?

I am not that person anymore,
I am so much more than that.

Talk to me

Talk to me in a kind voice,
and hold me as if I was going to break.
Nurture my soul
with words of wisdom
 and gentle whispers of hope.
Follow my heart and all its phases,
just like the moon;
knowing that even when you cannot see me,
it only means I am resting
and waiting for the new light
to shine on me again.

New beginnings

Let go of your past
by grieving the part of you that died.
Then, trust in the magic of new beginnings.

Distant memory

For the longest time, you occupied
all the space I had left inside my head:
Every tiny piece of my broken heart,
every fibre of my being,
every breath.
But I don't miss you anymore;
I miss how I felt in your arms.
I miss the thought of you.
I long for the day
you will finally be a distant memory.

Shelter

Within the impossibility of it all,
I will always give your soul a home.

To my daughters

As I look at you, my little ones, I see a universe, and all the stars and the magic of a life yet to unfold.

I listen to your little voices, and I can hear so much determination at such a young age.

Ride the rainbow of life, little ones. They will tell you at some point that you are not worth it, or that you must change, or that you're not enough. And I will be here to hold your hand, and to remind you that your worth is not determined by other people's opinions of you.

Shine like the brighter stars in the sky, and when you feel down, straighten up your crown, and remember how amazing you are.

Remember that I will always be here to catch you whenever you fall.

Who am I?

I always wanted to be the kind of woman
that you could love, be proud of
and hold when I felt scared.
I always wanted to be the kind of woman
who you thought was worth it.
I guess I had to figure out
that I was *always* worth it.
I didn't need your validation to feel whole,
and that is the kind of woman I always want to be.

The purple sky

There is a place,
a safe and warm zone
where I go to rest.

It's a place where I am never disappointed,
and I am always happy
and satisfied and whole.

It's a place where there's only love,
and where dreams become reality.

There are no boundaries of time and space.
I can get whatever I want.

I go there often.

It's a place where there is
a wonderful purplish light
just on the horizon.
where it is neither day nor night.

It's a place in between.

It's a place where I imagine the opposite to attract,
the impossible to happen, and the magic to sparkle.

Some people call it "dreams" – but sometimes I even
wonder if that is my true reality and what I live every day
is the dream.

For without dreams,
what are we?

What if?

What if all the pain I am feeling right now
was preparing me for something amazing?
What if all these *fires* surrounding me now
are just allowing me to realise
how strong I really am?

Believe

Look at yourself as though
you were looking at your own child.
Love her, nurture her,
and speak to her softly,
laughing at her silly mistakes
with no judgment.
Hold her tightly
until she can smile again.

The sandcastle

And then there was you,
stepping into and becoming
my entire world.
You got under my skin
and built an illusion
with your sweet and steady lies.
I forgot what I had
in my world before you,
all whilst you knit a new one;
crafting a wild house of cards.
You built it on sand
only for it to come crashing down
like a wave finding the shore.

Permission to change

Give yourself permission to change,
to evolve,
and to become
a different version of you.
Honour the old you,
as she took you right
to where you are now.
Allow your wings to open up
and fly to where you were
always meant to.

Love and prudence

Love and Prudence were having one of those endless arguments in which neither of them were winning.

"But I'm falling for you, and I'm so scared of getting hurt. I can't do this; I can't do this. How do I stop and make sure I won't get hurt?" cried Prudence to Love with desperation in her eyes.

Love was mad at Prudence for this, this much I know. Love wanted Prudence to lose herself to the madness, the desire and everything else that would come from him!

"But okay, what if I take this slowly and really hold myself and my feelings, so maybe I can take the good and will never experience hurt. Love, can you do this for me?"

Love began to lose his patience at such whining. How can Prudence be so blind? How could she stop herself from feeling what she was? Does she really believe that by not living the moment to the fullest she will not fall for him?

It was beyond anything he could comprehend, and frankly Love was beginning to resent Prudence!

Without falling for Love, Prudence would only experience half the good things she could, for it was Love itself that makes good things amazing. After all Craziness never minded, and her and Love were always the best of friends.

Love was thoughtful.

Risk was having none of this nonsense. He looked at Prudence in her eyes and said: "Take me! I'm here to bring you to the next level. If you don't take me, you'll never step outside your comfort zone, and therefore won't be able to see what's really out there."

"But Fear showed me" - said Prudence - "he came to my bed last night and had all these images to show me like a movie. Oh, it was horrible, tears, upset, Love tearing my heart out and shattered in a million pieces! Oh, I don't want that!"

Love was terribly angry at Fear now. He always did that! Never left anyone alone to fall for Love without any of these terrible things Fear was doing!

"I resent that!" - Fear said - "I don't show up if I'm not wanted. See if a teenager cares for me? They fall for you, Love, my dear friend. It's only when you, and only you, disappoint that I can come back later in life and show them what you are really made of!" said Fear to Love, as angry as ever.

Risk was still there, waiting to be taken. Love was silent now, and Fear looking the other way. Prudence was disheartened. Wisdom was watching the scene and took a deep sigh as he was always used to doing.

Then he spoke to them softly: "Prudence, you like walking, don't you? Can you always ensure there's no obstacle on your path? Can you always remove all the stones to make sure you do not fall?"

Prudence listened with interest but then said: "I could remove all the stones, and always watch my feet. Or I could choose a path I know there are no obstacles."

Wisdom smiled at Prudence and simply added: "What if you get a cramp in your leg and fall? Can you control that?"

"No, I cannot but I could stop walking," replied Prudence wanting to have her reasons listened to.

Wisdom then said to her: "Then you would stop living; stay still and watch life go by. Is this what you want?"

"And as for you, Love, I know you and Craziness are best of friends and will always travel together. However, you need to balance out and make sure Patience is involved. I haven't seen her today, where might she be?

Love, I know you take what you want, and once fallen for you there is no going back. But show Prudence all the things that come with you as she's scared: how you can make the heart race, and how you allow people's brains to change and see the loved one so differently; how you can make somebody literally ache when the other one is away, and how good it feels when the two people are finally together. That feeling that Prudence is so scared about is the most amazing one of all. Show Prudence this, so that she can take Risk and stop listening to Fear.

You see, to fall in love is something beyond anybody's control, much like a cramp in your leg. Or like a thunderstorm or a lunar eclipse.

To make something good about it, make sure you have your friend Courage beside you. Patience will show you the light if the chosen path is difficult. And Fear will fade away, this I can assure you.

And, Prudence, you will finally get to meet the most important person of your life: Happiness.

So - please - stop arguing."

Grace

I am going to navigate this new storm,
like I have so many storms before.
I am going to own it
with grace and vulnerability.
I will be patient with myself,
and wait
for this *new lesson* to be revealed.

Changes

I am not the same person anymore,
as so much in life has changed,
that on some days
even my heart beats differently.
As though my molecular structure
has also changed.
But I still dream, and I still believe,
and I still *hope*.

Sunflowers

Today I thought of sunflowers
and bright colours.
I even wore a yellow jumper
in an attempt to feel lighter.
I cleaned my home and tidied everywhere,
as if I was clearing my own emotional space
so I could somehow feel less overwhelmed.

I placed control on things I could control, like rearranging
flowers, and brushing my cat's fur.
It was like a lucid meditation. My hands were doing things
while my mind was dancing away in a long lost ballroom
filled with distant spectators and their sad eyes.

I thought of all the things that I have to go through, hover-
ing on the horizon of imaginary timelines that I can see
so clearly, and yet, cannot pinpoint exactly the days or
months of these future events.

My mind swirls with a deep sense of grief and loss trying
to grasp that small light that desperately wants to emerge,
somewhere in the future.

I thought of the world and how much more kindness we need, and thought of how unfair things can be and I swam in a pool of self-pity nearly paralysed with fear.

So I kept my body moving and hands busy while all the emotions crystallised in salty and warm tears, a small relief.

I thought of sunflowers today.

The idea

Sometimes I wonder if I was
really in love with you
more than the idea itself
of being in love with you.

Fixing you

Maybe the whole purpose of meeting you
was to fix you.
Maybe the whole purpose of you
breaking me so badly
was for me to realise that I could fully fix myself.
And for that,
I am strangely thankful to you.

Motherhood

That moment when you are finally falling asleep,
I look at your perfect little face,
with that little mouth slightly open,
and hand holding mine.
That moment exactly
is when I feel most at peace.
I feel the entire universe right there
and everything suddenly makes sense.
My heart slows down
and fills with the kind of love,
that takes my breath away.
That is the moment where nothing,

nothing else matters.

Out cold

You touched my heart in ways
I didn't think possible.
You also left me out, stone cold
on the bare floor,
in a way I never imagined
anyone ever could...

She is all the stars
on the darkest nights.
She is the warmth
of the midday sun
and the calmest
of still waters.
She is the shelter in the storm,
and the gentle caress that soothes
the most troubled soul.
She is the lighthouse in the dark,
and the compass
that guides me home.

My sister

Heavy heart

This heart of mine is heavy
and full of dust.
I am no longer waiting for anyone
to clean it up.
I am learning,
Oh, I am learning...

Perspective

There is beauty in contradictions,
there is light in the shadows,
and there is healing in pain.
When we shift perspective,
we finally see
what we were always meant to see.

Believe

Believe in yourself, little one.
Only the bravest heart can truly
conquer this world.

Chains

I have buried these emotions
for the longest time.
Fear was the only one that made sense
because I gave myself permission to feel it.
I couldn't allow you to break my heart again.
So Instead, I kept it locked
in the tightest of chains,
and threw away the key.

Another day

Owl is singing again this morning;
the bird chorus following him in an effortless concert.
They remind me that they are alive, and so am I.
They celebrate a new morning, welcoming new life;
another opportunity to change something.

Another day;
they are talking to me about love and renewal
as the world slowly wakes, and I stir in bed with sleepy
eyes and heavy heart.

They remind me that the reason why I feel so much pain
is love.

If I didn't love as much as I do, I wouldn't feel all of this.
Owl reminded me of that this morning.

Would you?

Would you stay if I asked you to stay?
Would you hold me and tell me everything will be ok?
Would you understand my silences if I didn't speak?
Would you replace these holes in my heart with flowers?
Would you see beauty in my newly formed scars?
Would you accept my need for space and
my endless contradictions?

Would you hold on to me?

Dawn

I keep waiting and hoping
for the next dawn
to be ours.

Simply us

I wanted you to choose us
above everything else;
above the unfeasibility of life,
above any conventions.
Us: simply us.

I was never asking for forever.
I was just asking for *now*.

Hope

It's not about pretending that dark times don't exist;
It is about believing that darkness will not
last forever.

4:04AM Thoughts

I dreamt of you again tonight,
or were you there in my bedroom
calling for me?
I often wonder where you are,
as I can feel you so close to me
as if death was only a mere passage
to a different form of life;
one where we communicate differently,
through emotions and dreams
and silent conversations.
Through tears and imaginary hugs,
with energy and intuition.
Grief, they say, is only love that doesn't
know where to go, trapped in a hollow chest.
What if I could trap this love on this very piece of paper
so that I could always find you again
in all my verses?

What if I could make these memories immortal,
reliving them every time I see you
in my rhymes, smiling sweetly
as if time had not passed,
erasing time and space?
Giving myself permission to imagine

what we would be today...
It's 4.04am again,
and the clock stares at me,
energy flowing through my veins
asking me to pick up my pen and write.

I must oblige now.

Acknowledgments

A massive thank you to Wren Coaching for allowing me to believe in myself, to find the courage to finally publish this book and realise my dream, because the only limits are the ones we create in our minds.

To my beautiful daughters for being my number one fans and asking to read some of my poems as bedtime stories.

To my best friend Nicola for creating the title of this book! To my family and friends, for believing in me and encouraging me to carry on.

To Elizabeth Spary, my amazing illustrator and friend, for her patience and incredible vision in bringing my poems to life.

A special thanks to Alix Klingenberg for being my first trusted reader giving me invaluable advice and support.

To Stefanie Briar for taking the time to review and edit my manuscript I am forever grateful and in awe of her incredible insights, effort, kindness and friendship.

To Purple Phoenix Poetry for supporting the management of the launch of the book.

To my brother Emmanuel for helping with the formatting and final publishing, I am forever grateful.

To the Instagram community for their endless support in my writing journey.

About the author

Barbara Gianquitto is a debut author who writes about love, heartbreak and self discovery. Born in Italy, she's a true advocate for mental health and women empowerment.

As a Reiki healer she is a great believer in energy and connections and that everything truly happens for a reason. Barbara has a bachelor's degree in Communication and Psychology, and is a certified Neuro Linguistic practitioner and coach.

Barbara currently lives in the North West of the United Kingdom with her two daughters and her cat Milly.

You can find more of Barbara's work on Instagram on @bg_babsauthor, on Facebook BarbaraNGianquitto and on her website www.barbaragianquitto.com